The Wallace Collection
general guide

The Trustees of the Wallace Collection
Manchester Square, London W1M 6BN
1986

Front cover: Boucher **Madame de Pompadour** (P418)
Back cover: A.-C. Boulle **Toilet mirror** (F50) detail
Title page: The Wallace of Craigie Crest used by
Sir Richard Wallace

Set in Linotron Baskerville by SX Composing
Printed by Perivan

1st Edition 1982
2nd Edition (revised) 1984
3rd Edition (revised 1986)

Contents

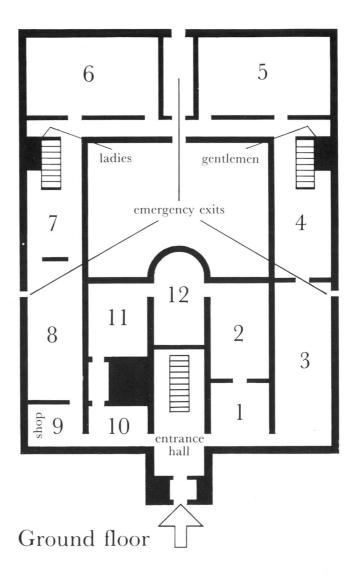

Ground floor

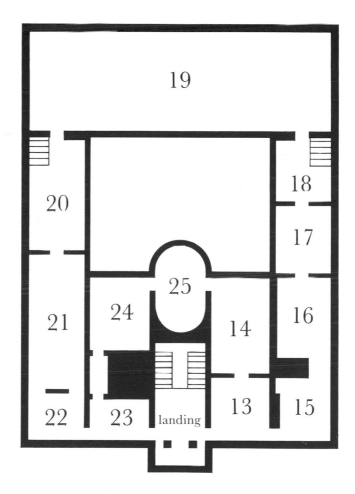

First floor

Foreword

This revised edition of the *General Guide* describes the Collection as it has been redisplayed in 1982, following a period of six years of building works at Hertford House. The contents differ in two principal respects from previous editions. Firstly the armouries, contained in Galleries 5 to 8, are here only mentioned, there now being a separate *Guide to the Armouries* of the Wallace Collection. Secondly, following the publication in 1981 of *The Founders of the Wallace Collection* by Peter Hughes, the history of the founders has been shortened.

John Ingamells

March 1982

Director

Explanation

The Galleries are described in numerical order. The visitor will find Gallery numbers fixed above each doorway. Galleries 1 to 12 are on the ground floor, 13 to 25 on the first floor.

All references to individual works of art are accompanied by their inventory numbers to facilitate their identification and to accord with the catalogues of the various sections of the Collection. The catalogues currently available are listed on p. 85. Some sections of the Collection (e.g. Objects of Art and Sèvres Porcelain) have no catalogue at present available.

The following dates of French rulers may be useful:

Charles IX	1560–74	Louis XV	1723–74
Henri III	1574–89	Louis XVI	1774–92
Henri IV	1589–1610	Convention	1792–5
Louis XIII	1610–43	Directoire	1795–9
Louis XIV	1643–1715	Consulate	1799–1804
Régence	1715–23	Napoleon I	1804–15

Introduction

The Founders

The Wallace Collection was bequeathed to the British Nation by Lady Wallace in 1897. She was the widow of Sir Richard Wallace, the illegitimate son of the 4th Marquess of Hertford. Her bequest, magnificent as it was, accounted for only half a collection which had been formed in the nineteenth century principally by her husband and by the 3rd and 4th Marquesses of Hertford. It had been gathered in London and in Paris where the 4th Marquess and Wallace lived most of their lives, and where both are now buried in the Père-Lachaise cemetery. Lady Wallace, who was French, bequeathed only those works of art in the main rooms of Hertford House in London; the considerable collection of French furniture, sculpture and tapestries which remained in Paris was eventually sold, in 1914, to the dealer Jacques Seligmann. Many of the items are now in American museums.

Both the 1st and 2nd Marquesses of Hertford had followed successful diplomatic careers and had made advantageous marriages, factors which facilitated the creation of the Marquisate of Hertford in 1793. Neither was particularly noted as a collector of works of art, though it appears that the 1st Marquess acquired several Canalettos, including the two fine views across the Bacino in Venice, and the 2nd Marquess purchased some notable English portraits, including the *Nelly O'Brien* by Reynolds. He was also given Gainsborough's full-length *Mrs 'Perdita' Robinson* by the Prince Regent, perhaps to compensate for the way in which the Prince usurped the attentions of the second Marchioness. An inventory taken on her death in 1834 shows that Hertford House was then furnished with French boulle furniture, bronzes, Sèvres porcelain and some miniatures, as well as English portraits.

Her only surviving child, Francis Seymour-Conway, had succeeded as the 3rd Marquess of Hertford in 1822. In 1798 he had married an Italian beauty, Maria Fagnani, daughter of the Marchesa Fagnani, a former dancer, by the notorious 4th Duke of Queensberry ('Old Q') who left her a considerable fortune, as did the Duke's close friend George Selwyn, in the belief that he too had a claim to her paternity. The Hertford family was now exceedingly rich; they already owned property in Ireland at Lisburn, County Antrim, Conway Castle in Wales, Ragley Hall in Warwickshire, Sudbourn Hall in Suffolk, and Old Q's bequest added houses in Piccadilly to their London residences in Grosvenor Street and Manchester Square. The 3rd Marquess added more; he acquired Dorchester House (on the site of the present Dorchester Hotel) and built the exotic St Dunstan's Villa in Regent's Park (demolished in 1937).

His Marchioness meanwhile had settled in Paris, while he led an increasingly disreputable life in London. It was the flamboyance of his later years which led to his characterisation as a sinister rake by Thackeray (Lord Steyne in *Vanity Fair*) and Disraeli (Lord Monmouth in *Coningsby*). The Marquess had belonged to the circle of the Prince Regent whom he had advised on the collecting of works of art. In 1822 he was made a Knight of the Garter. He was himself a perceptive collector, as the inventory of Dorchester House, taken on his death in 1842, makes clear. He bought particularly fine Dutch cabinet pictures, including Rembrandt's *Landscape with a coach* and Netscher's *The Lace Maker*, miniatures, boulle and Sèvres-plaqued French furniture, French and Italian bronzes, and Sèvres porcelain. Today his finest acquisition might be considered the *Perseus and Andromeda* by Titian, an exceptional purchase for a man whose taste was essentially that of a *fermier-général* in the reign of Louis XVI.

Richard Seymour-Conway, his only surviving legitimate child, succeeded as 4th Marquess of Hertford in 1842. He was a highly intelligent but cynical man who, after an English education and a brief period of military and diplomatic service, settled in Paris. He had acquired apartments at 2 rue Laffitte in 1829, and in 1835 he purchased Bagatelle, a château in the Bois de Boulogne, originally built for the comte d'Artois (later Charles X of France). Unlike his father he found collecting a wholly absorbing occupation, perhaps the only activity capable of overcoming his natural spleen. 'He would not even have drawn aside his curtain to see a revolution pass in the street below', a friend said of him, and yet, as an intimate friend of Napoleon III, he was well aware of political events. The 4th Marquess never married, but at the age of eighteen he became the father of Richard (Wallace) by one Mrs Agnes Jackson, and Mme Suzanne Oger was to be the constant companion of his later years.

He had inherited a significant collection, as we have seen, but he increased it on a spectacular scale so that it became one of European repute. He assembled a gallery of seventeenth-century European paintings of outstanding quality with such works as Rubens's *Rainbow landscape*, Velazquez's *Lady with a fan*, Rembrandt's *Titus*, Van Dyck's *Philippe le Roy*, Poussin's *Dance to the music of Time*, and landscapes by Claude, Rosa, Ruisdael and Hobbema. He continued his father's enthusiasm for the *ancien régime* in acquiring paintings by Boucher, Watteau, Fragonard and Greuze, furniture by Gaudreau, Cressent, Riesener, Carlin and Weisweiler, Sèvres porcelain, miniatures, Gobelins and Beauvais tapestries, and fine sculpture in bronze and marble. Nor did he neglect contemporary French painters, such as Meissonier, Decamps, Delaroche and Horace Vernet. In all these separate fields his taste was for *pleasing* works of art; he disliked, he said, portraits of old men, scenes of violence, all primitive art of the fourteenth and fifteenth centuries, and any hint of realism (thus he neglected the works of Daumier, Courbet, Millet and Manet, for example). The quiet composure and soft colouring of an attractive Madonna by Murillo he considered far preferable. The immense contribution of the 4th Marquess to the Wallace Collection conveys a sense of luxury and refined pleasure which the visitor can easily appreciate today.

The 4th Marquess died at Bagatelle in August 1870, attended by Richard Wallace. Within weeks the Prussian army reached Paris. Wallace had been brought up in Paris from the age of six by the 3rd Marchioness; he became his father's secretary and an increasingly knowledgeable connoisseur of the arts. As an illegitimate son he could not, of course, inherit the Marquisate which passed to a second cousin but, to the surprise of many, he did inherit all the unentailed property and fortune, including the Paris and London residences with their collections. Before he could enjoy his inheritance however he found himself in a besieged and then insurgent Paris. As if to redeem his father's insouciance Wallace indulged in lavish charitable work, including the endowment of the Hertford British Hospital, the provision of numerous field ambulances, and the gift to the City of Paris of some fifty drinking fountains, known to this day as *Wallaces* (one is now sited in front of Hertford House). In all he was said to have spent two-and-a-half million francs on such philanthropy, for which he received a Baronetcy in December 1871. In February he had married Julie Castelnau, already the mother of his thirty-year-old son. Early in 1872 Sir Richard and Lady Wallace left Paris to settle in London where they determined to convert Hertford House to accommodate that part of their huge collection which was brought over from Paris. While such conversions were taking place the Wallaces lived in another Hertford property, 105 Piccadilly, and the collection was exhibited from 1872 to 1875 in the newly-opened Bethnal Green Museum. It caused astonishment and wonder.

Wallace made two significant additions to the collection. In 1871 he purchased the collection of arms, armour and Renaissance decorative art which had been formed by the comte de Nieuwerkerke, Napoleon III's *surintendant des beaux-arts,* and a large and choice selection of arms and armour from the famous collection of Sir Samuel Meyrick (1786–1848). He thus extended the historical scope of the collection back to the fourteenth century. Wallace also acquired a small collection of illuminated manuscript cuttings and early

Italian paintings from the vicomte de Tauzia in 1872, and he bought maiolica, Sèvres and some other paintings, including Fragonard's *Pierrot*.

The Wallace Collection was practically complete by 1880 and the Hertford House visitors' book lists many distinguished guests who came to admire it. It would seem, however, that Wallace was never entirely absorbed into London society, despite his strenuous efforts as MP for Lisburn and as a generous Trustee of the National Gallery. The circumstances of his birth and his wife's strict adherence to the French language cannot have helped his cause. He died at Bagatelle, in the same room as his father, in July 1890. His son Edmond (1840–87) predeceased him, but left four illegitimate children whose descendants are still living.

The idea of giving the collection to the British Nation had first been mentioned by the 4th Marquess in 1867, but nothing came of it. In the 1880s Wallace had approached the Treasury with the same idea, but his stipulation that Hertford House should be acquired as a suitable site was then rejected and the negotiation collapsed. Lady Wallace, despite her apparent indifference to English language and society, loyally observed her husband's wishes in making her bequest, the first condition of which was

> That the Government . . . shall agree to give a site in a central part of London, and build thereon a special museum to contain the said Collection which shall be kept together, unmixed with other objects of art, and shall be styled *The Wallace Collection*.

Ironically, in view of Wallace's earlier experience, the Government decided to purchase the lease of Hertford House from Lady Wallace's residuary legatee, John Murray Scott, and the museum was opened on 22 June 1900 by the Prince of Wales, the future Edward VII. Lady Wallace's wish that the Collection should remain 'unmixed with other objects of art' has meant that no works of art may be added to or borrowed from the Collection.

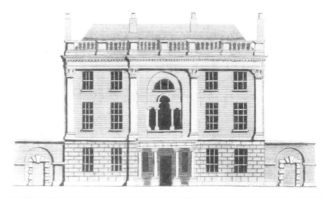

Manchester House *c.*1788
(engraving, Westminster City
Libraries, Marylebone Archives
and Local History Department)

Manchester House 1815
(Wallace Collection archives)

Hertford House *c.*1900

12

Hertford House

The home of the Wallace Collection was built as Manchester
House by one Joshua Brown between 1776 and 1788 for the
4th Duke of Manchester. He owned the square which is still
named after him and which then offered good duck shooting
nearby. It was a five-bay stuccoed house with giant pilasters,
a rusticated ground floor and a fine Venetian window on the
first floor. After the Duke's death in 1788 the House was
leased as the Spanish Embassy from 1791 to 1795; the street
to the east of the house is still called Spanish Place.

In 1797 the lease was acquired by the 2nd Marquess of
Hertford who, by 1807, had added two first-floor rooms on
each wing and a conservatory outside the Venetian window.
Manchester House was the principal residence of the 2nd
Marquess and his Marchioness. The Prince Regent was a
frequent guest and must often have sat in what is now Gallery
25 making eyes at the ample figure of the Marchioness. Two
years after her death in 1834 the 3rd Marquess let the house,
together with some of the English portraits, as the French
Embassy. Guizot described it in 1840 as 'a large building
between a little gravelled court and a damp garden, with a
handsome ground floor well arranged for official and cere-
monious purposes, but bare and inconvenient in the first
storey, for domestic life'.

In 1851 the Embassy departed and there followed a period
of twenty years in which the house, now owned by the 4th
Marquess of Hertford, lay empty save for an expectant
domestic staff and an ever increasing number of works of art,
comprising those transferred from Dorchester House and
other London residences, and those purchased in London by
the 4th Marquess of Hertford through his agents.

In 1871 Sir Richard Wallace determined to settle in Man-
chester Square, and he renamed his property Hertford
House. He commissioned an obscure architect, Thomas
Ambler, to extend it in order to accommodate that part of the
collection brought over from Paris. Between 1872 and 1875
Ambler completed the three sides of an inner quadrangle

with stabling, coach-houses and a Minton-tiled smoking room on the ground floor, and top-lit galleries on the first floor. He also reworked the main façade of the house by raising the east and west wings to the full height of the central block, modifying the conservatory on the first floor, and changing the stucco to the red brick seen today.

Between 1897 and 1900 the Office of Works converted the house into a public museum. The stabling, coach-houses and smoking room became exhibition galleries, private rooms on the west side of the first floor became an additional top-lit gallery, and office and workshop accommodation was introduced on the second and third floors. The house has since undergone a number of minor modifications; three small exhibition rooms were built on the second floor in 1913–5, only to prove impracticable and to be used for storage purposes; a staff lift was installed in 1922; the Minton tiles were removed from the former smoking room in 1937 when several dividing walls were removed and doorways blocked up in other exhibition rooms (such changes are noted in the ensuing guide).

Between 1976 and 1981 the installation of air-conditioning necessitated further structural changes, including new, lower, ceilings for the first-floor top-lit galleries. The two air-handling units have been accommodated in the front vaults (for the ground-floor rooms) and in the second-floor storage galleries (for the first-floor rooms). The complex installation was completed with a minimum of interference to the appearance of the exhibition rooms.

The House was redecorated at this time and, following Wallace's practice, carpeting was introduced into the domestic rooms, partly to distinguish them from the purpose-built exhibition galleries. The pattern was derived from photographs of Wallace's first-floor carpet.

Entrance Hall

A Day Lodge and a Night Lodge by the iron gates facing Manchester Square, built by Ambler in 1872–5, were dismantled in 1897–1900. A simple open porch was extended forward with a porte-cochère in 1897–1900 in order to accommodate the cloakroom, and this area was again modified in 1982. From 1900 to 1976 the sales area was behind the main staircase. The lanterns each side of the staircase were introduced in 1981.

On the right is displayed a trophy of eighteenth and nineteenth-century Oriental arms arranged around an eighteenth-century Indian shield of rhinoceros's hide. On the left, above the chimney-piece, hangs **The Prince of Wales** (P563) by **Hoppner** which was presented to the 3rd Marquess of Hertford by the sitter; the frame bears the Prince's crest of three feathers. On each side of it are Louis XVI **wall-lights** (F370, F371) made for Marie-Antoinette's *salon des jeux* at Fontainebleau. On the chimneypiece stands a fine Louis XVI **clock** with the figure of Clio (F267), the movement by **Ferdinand Berthoud**.

Mantel Clock French (F267)

Behind and on each side of the staircase hang a number of pictures having close associations with the Hertford family. They include portraits by **Reynolds** of the **4th Duke of**

Queensberry (P561) and of two of the daughters of the 1st Marquess of Hertford (P31, P33).

Turning to the right the visitor enters Gallery 1.

Gallery 1

Originally the Front State Room with an additional door leading back to the Entrance Hall. In 1900 two arches were introduced into the north dividing wall. In 1937 this wall was dismantled and the additional door filled in. In 1976 the present north wall was installed. The light-fitting was introduced in 1978, replacing a Caffiéri chandelier now in Gallery 14.

This Gallery contains eighteenth and nineteenth-century English pictures, including works by Reynolds, Lawrence, Wilkie and Landseer. On the west wall hangs a coronation portrait of **Queen Victoria** (P564) by the American artist **Thomas Sully**, a version of a full-length now in a private collection in America. Next to it hangs **Lawrence's** well-

Lawrence The Countess of Blessington (P558)

known Countess of Blessington (P558). There are also some enamel miniatures by Henry Bone after Reynolds and Madame Vigée Lebrun.

The furniture is French from the Louis XVI period and includes two tulip-wood corner cupboards (F273, F274) made by Gilles Joubert for the comte d'Artois at Versailles, and another pair of wall-lights from Fontainebleau (F372, F373, see Entrance Hall). The nineteenth-century French pier-glass (F442) was introduced in 1982.

On each side of the chimney-piece stand marble busts; to the left Charles I (S23) by L. F. Roubiliac, and to the right Queen Caroline (S24) by J. M. Rysbrack. Both originally belonged to George Selwyn (see p. 8).

Leaving through the north doorway the visitor enters Gallery 2.

Gallery 2

Originally the Back State Room, decorated with white and gilt wood panelling (boiseries) in the Louis XVI style and three pier-glasses, and with two additional doors leading back to the Entrance Hall and to Gallery 3. The boiseries and mirrors were removed in 1937 when the additional doorways were also filled in.

This Gallery contains fine boulle furniture, Sèvres porcelain and seventeenth-century European paintings which include the Centurion Cornelius (P86), famous in the nineteenth century as a fine Rembrandt but now considered to be the work of one of his followers, and the beautiful Marriage of the Virgin (P14) by Murillo.

On each side of the chimney-piece (F459), a nineteenth-century copy of that made by Caffiéri for the son of Louis XV at Versailles in 1747, are displayed four Louis XIV bronze figures of the Seasons (S172–5) mounted on two pairs of boulle pedestals. On the chimneypiece stands the celebrated early Louis XV mantel clock, *la nymphe à la coquille* (F93), with the gilt-bronze figures of Venus and Cupid. Between the win-

A.-C. Boulle **Wardrobe** (F62) detail

dows on the north wall stands the large **wardrobe** (F62) from the workshop of **A.-C. Boulle,** while to the left stands the **pedestal clock** (F43) mounted with the figures of *Love triumphing over Time.* Against the west wall stands a **chest of drawers** (*commode*) (F39), with marquetry designed in the manner of Jean Berain (1637–1711). The very fine gilt-bronze **chandelier** (F83) by **Jacques Caffiéri** is dated 1751.

Jacques Caffiéri **Chandelier** (F83)

In the centre of the Gallery are two cases containing porcelain from the French royal factory at Sèvres. Case 1 includes pieces with the turquoise blue ground colour introduced in 1752. The pair of **flower pots** (XXV A10–11) with sculpted dolphins at the sides were made in 1756; each pot is in two sections, the upper to contain plants growing in earth, the lower for water. The unique pair of **saucepans** (XXII A36–7) with delicately sculpted handles of scrolls and foliage are dated 1759.

Saucepan Sèvres porcelain (XXII 36)

Case 2 contains examples of the dark-blue ground colour. Many of the pieces are painted with pastoral scenes in the manner of Boucher and one vase (XXII 15) is decorated with *The Peepshow* after Boucher on the front and with a trophy of children's toys on the reverse.

The visitor should now turn back through Gallery 1 and turn left into Gallery 3.

Gallery 3

Originally divided into two State Rooms, the south containing Wallace's paintings by Canaletto and Guardi, the north being his Sixteenth-Century Room. In 1897–1900 the two east windows at the south end were made, and the dividing wall was dismantled and replaced by two free-standing fluted columns, removed in 1937. Wallace's marble south chimney-piece, now in Gallery 15, was also removed in 1937 to be replaced by the present wooden structure made to match the proportions of the north chimney-piece. The chandeliers were installed in 1979 and are based on those originally used by Wallace.

This Gallery contains paintings and objects of art dating from the fourteenth to the eighteenth centuries. To the left of the door on entering stands the very fine sixteenth-century bronze bust of **Charles IX of France** (S154) by **Germain Pilon**.

Beyond the south chimney-piece wall-case A contains a

19

miscellaneous collection of European sixteenth and seventeenth-century objects of art. These include, on the left, an iron and gilt-bronze **casket** (III K563) made at Augsburg *c*.1550, and four pieces of Portuguese late-sixteenth-century silver-gilt, of which a **ewer and basin** (XII A110–11), in the centre, bear the arms of Pius IV, Pope from 1559 to 1565. To the right another **ewer and basin** (III F279–80) of copper enamelled in blue and white and bearing coats of arms (including those of the Ciacchi family of Florence) were made in Venice in the sixteenth century.

Above the case hangs the portrait of a **Gentleman** (P26) by **Frans Pourbus** the elder.

Wall-case B contains a fine collection of Limoges enamels including, in the centre, a series of twenty-four **plaques** (III F250) ascribed to **Jean II Pénicaud** representing scenes connected with the Passion after woodcuts by Dürer; to the left a small portrait of **Henri d'Albret** (III F255), grandfather of Henri IV of France, is signed by **L. Limousin**. A large oval **dish** decorated with *Apollo and the Muses* (III F268), the scenes

Pilon **Charles IX of France** (S154) detail

Torrigiano **Head of Christ** (S7) detail

taken from Raphael's painting of *Parnassus*, is by **Martial Reymond**, and to the right the fine dish (III F270) is painted in grisaille with a design taken from Raphael's *Triumph of Galatea*.

Above the north chimney-piece, which is Italian and dates from *c*.1500, is set the marble **Head of Christ** (S7) by **Pietro Torrigiano**, carved between 1511–20 and originally set in the Islip Chapel in Westminster Abbey. Below it, on the chimney-piece, stands the early-sixteenth-century Florentine terracotta of **S. John the Baptist** (S55), attributed to the **Master of the David and S. John Statuettes**.

Dish with Apollo and the Muses
Limoges enamel (III F268) detail

Wall-case C shows a collection of glass. The majority of pieces were made in Venice or in the Venetian manner (*façon de Venise*) in the sixteenth and seventeenth centuries. The principal techniques are represented: colourless glass (*cristallo*), the use of opaque white glass canes (*vetro a filigrana*), mould-blowing, and ice glass. There is also a good range of decorative techniques, including enamelling, gilding, diamond-point engraving, and applied reliefs. The earliest

Goblet Venetian glass
(XXV B92)

Shutters of a Triptych
French enamel (XII A68)

piece, to the left, is a mid-fourteenth-century Syrian **mosque lamp** (XXV B94). Of particular interest are the Venetian 'chalcedony' **goblet** (XXV B92) of *c*.1500, the sixteenth-century Venetian **tazza** (XXV B72) of *cristallo* glass with a mould-blown lion, and the French sixteenth-century **glass** of chalice form (XXV B96), probably made by Venetians working in France.

Above the case hangs the **Allegorical Love Feast** (P531) by **Pieter Pourbus**, father of Frans Pourbus whose portrait of a gentleman has already been noticed.

On the north wall, to the right of the doorway, are two interesting fragments from fifteenth-century altarpieces; the **S. Roch** by **Carlo Crivelli** (P527), and **The Archangel Michael** by **Hans Memlinc** (P528).

On the east wall beyond the first window is the charming **Young Cicero reading** (P538) by **Vincenzo Foppa**, once part of the fifteenth-century wall decorations of the Banco Mediceo in Milan. Below it stands a sixteenth-century French carved walnut **cupboard** (F10).

Wall-case D suggests a nineteenth-century *cabinet de curiosités*. Particularly curious are the late-sixteenth-century Italian rock crystal **tazza** (I A14), the German **coconut cup** (III F271) and the German **warrior** formed of two baroque pearls (I A35) from the same period.

Wall-case E contains an important, essentially Medieval collection of ecclesiastical works of art. Of outstanding interest are the small **shutters of a triptych** of translucent enamel on gold (XII A68) showing on the reverse (reflected in the mirror) Charlemagne and S. Louis of France and, on the obverse, Pierre II duc de Bourbon (d. 1503) with S. Peter, and his wife Anne of France with S. Anne; the designs of the donors correspond to the wings of the famous triptych in Moulins cathedral by the Maître de Moulins, while the figure of Charlemagne may derive from a painting by the Master's studio now in the National Gallery, London. Of other pieces, the **Burial of a Bishop** (III N286) is a detached high-relief in gilt-bronze made in Limoges in the thirteenth century; the standing **cup and cover** (XII A112B) of parcel-gilt

22

silver decorated with translucent enamels was made in Augsburg c.1600.

There are four cases standing in the centre of the gallery. Case 1, nearest the windows at the south end, contains a collection of seventeenth-century bronze, ivory and boxwood statuettes from Italy and northern Europe showing the influence of **Giovanni da Bologna**.

Case 2 contains a collection of waxes and includes many Italian, French and German portraits from the sixteenth to the eighteenth centuries. On the west side are fine miniatures of the **Archduke Ernst of Austria** (S434) by A. Abondio, **Don Garcia dei Medici** (S427), and the **duc and duchesse de Mercoeur** (S439, S440). At the north end is the large **Mary Magdalen washing Christ's feet** (S463), probably German work from the early-seventeenth century; on each side of it are two late-sixteenth century Italian figures of **Judith** (S461) and **Dido** (S462), and above them is the **Adoration of the Magi** (S459), a late-sixteenth-century Saxon work in which the figures are portraits of the Electoral family of Saxony, with its contemporary gilt-copper case. On the east side is the portrait of a **Lady** (S453) by **B. L. Wimmer** dated 1787, and a series of four eighteenth-century portraits (S419–22) based on earlier pictures in the Uffizi Gallery, Florence. In the south compartment is the full-length **Ulrich, Grundherr von Altenhann and Weiherhauss** (S449) by **G. Holdermann** dated 1627, flanked with two eighteenth-century genre scenes (S464, S465) by **G. F. Pieri**. The raised centre section contains a selection of European sixteenth and seventeenth-century silver and silver-gilt work, including a **steeple cup and cover** (XII L195) made in London in 1613–4.

Case 3 (the visitor should lift the covers) contains an important collection of illuminated manuscript cuttings from the fourteenth to the sixteenth centuries, taken from Medieval and Renaissance books and framed in the nineteenth century. Of particular quality are the **Galeazzo Sforza, Duke of Milan, praying for Victory** (21) by **Cristoforo da Preda** dated 1477, and the two scenes from **Boëthius** (1, 2) attributed

Master of Coëtivy Boethius
consoled by Philosophy (M320)
detail

to the fifteenth-century French **Maître de Coëtivy** (in the west and south compartments respectively). The origin of the miniature is suggested by the fifteenth-century Ferrarese **Roundel with a Scholar's portrait** (19) on the east side. The earliest fragments are the two **illuminated capital letters** from Pisa of the mid-fourteenth century (10, 11) in the north compartment. In the raised centre section is a collection of north European **boxwood carvings** and **bronzes** dating from the sixteenth and seventeenth centuries.

Case 4 contains three important north Italian terracottas; the **bust of a boy** (S54) is attributed to **A. Rossellino**; the statuette of **Giovanni dei Medici (called** *delle Bande Nere*) (S57), is attributed to **Niccolo Tribolo**, and the **Head of S. John the Baptist** (S6) is attributed to **A. Solario**.

The visitor continues on through the doorway leading to Gallery 4.

Gallery 4

Built by Ambler in 1872–5 as a Minton-tiled smoking room with a street entrance on the east side and three arches at the north end, the left one leading to the back stairs to the first floor. The street door was filled in, and the back staircase modified, in 1897–1900. From 1900–14 the gallery contained metal-work and sculpture, and from 1914–37 the Oriental armoury. In 1937 the tiles were removed. In 1978 the north-east alcove was opened up to reveal the only surviving Minton tiles.

This Gallery maintains the character of Gallery 3, showing principally objects of art from the fifteenth to the seventeenth centuries. The furniture includes three sixteenth-century French carved wood **cupboards** (F8, F9, F11), and a carved **dresser** (F14).

On either side of the doorway are two paintings of the **Virgin and Child** (P8, P10) by **Bernardino Luini** and two

24

bronze **candlesticks** (S138, S139) supported by life-size figures of cupids by **Ferdinando Tacca**. Above the door is set a French eighteenth-century bronze **relief** (S155) from the antique marble in the Louvre known as *Les Danseuses Borghèse*.

Between the windows on the west side stand two fine seventeenth-century bronze fire dogs, **Juno controlling the winds** (S162) and **Jupiter victorious over the Titans** (S161), by **Michel Anguier** after models by A. Algardi; they once belonged to the Grand Dauphin, eldest son of Louis XIV, and later to the French crown.

Set in the tiled alcove in the north-east corner is the marble **Love Triumphant** (S27), a copy made in 1871 of the eighteenth-century piece by **J.-P.-A. Tassaert** now in the Louvre; Wallace commissioned the copy and paid for the restoration of the damaged original in the same year.

On the east wall three wall-cases contain sixteenth and seventeenth-century **earthenwares** and **stonewares** from Italy, Spain, France, Germany and Turkey. Case A shows Italian lustred maiolica. One item (C27) shows the distinctive silvery yellows of Deruta, and another (C66), decorated with the *Bath of Maidens* by **Maestro Giorgio Andreoli** in April 1525, shows the rich red lustre of Gubbio.

Wall-case B contains tin-glazed **earthenwares**, Spanish Hispano-Moresque pieces with brilliant metallic lustres and Italian **maiolica** made at Urbino. Most famous of the Urbino potters was **Fra Xanto Avelli da Rovigo** who painted in 1533 the **dish** with the *Triumph of Alcyone* and the arms of the Michiel and Gritti families of Venice (C89). The vast **wine-cooler** (C107) was made in Urbino in 1574, probably for Cosimo I de' Medici.

Wall-case C shows **Turkish (Isnik) wares** with the colours and patterns which inspired the much later Minton tiles seen in the alcove in this gallery. The French **lead-glazed earthenwares** were made by **Bernard Palissy** (1510–90), or by his followers. Two **dishes** (C173, C174) on display are good examples of his applied natural detail showing snakes, lizards, shells and foliage, and two (C169, C170) of the exotic

Dish Isnik earthenware
(C200) detail

Dish with the Triumph of Alcyone
Urbino maiolica (C89) detail

Dish Palissy earthenware (C173)

glazes which give a mottled effect similar to marble or tortoiseshell. The German stonewares include the white salt-glazed **jug with silver cover** (C187) made at Siegburg in the late-sixteenth century. Some stonewares of the same period, shown with contemporary pieces of pewter, demonstrate how both metal-workers and potters relied on similar sources for decoration.

Above the wall-cases hang three nineteenth-century French paintings, by **Baron Leys, Robert-Fleury** and **Jacquand** (P275, P361, P648), each with a subject from sixteenth-century European history.

There are three cases standing in the centre of the gallery. Case 1, at the south end nearest the entrance door, shows on the east side a collection of coins and medals. Particularly noteworthy are those of **Gianfrancesco Gonzaga, Marquess of Mantua** (S328) by **Pisanello; Sigismondo Pandolfo Malatesta** (S329) by **Matteo dei Pasti** dated 1446, and the lead

Pisanello **Gianfrancesco Gonzaga** (S328)

26

medal of the **Emperor Charles V** (S400) designed by **Dürer** for the City of Nuremberg in 1521. On the west side is a collection of wood and ivory carvings, including the very fine leaf from a **diptych** (S249) by the **Master of the Mège Diptych** who worked in Paris between 1325 and 1350, and three late-seventeenth-century **ivories** by **C. D. Schenk** (**Man of Sorrows**, S257), **François Bossuit** (**Toilet of Bathsheba**, S263), and **Dominikus Stainhart** (**Diana and Calisto**, S265). In the south compartment are two curious antiquities, the **Bell of S. Mura** (III J498) probably dating from the tenth century, and the **Horn of S. Hubert** (III J499) of the later-fifteenth century encrusted with gesso, painted and gilt, and decorated with *champlevé* enamel.

Master of the Mège Diptych
Leaf of a Diptych (S249)

Giovanni Fonduli Seated Nymph (S72)

Case 2 shows a number of important Italian Renaissance bronzes and statuettes. The distinguished late-fifteenth-century **Seated Nymph** (S72) is signed OPVS IO CRE, thought to be **Giovanni Fonduli**. Two early-sixteenth-century **bronzes** of youths in movement (S73, S74) are attributed to **Vittor**

Francesco da Sant'Agata
Hercules (S273)

Camelio. They relate stylistically to the very fine and rare box-wood statuette of **Hercules** (S273) by **Francesco da Sant'Agata**, signed and dated 1520.

Case 3 contains in the south compartment Italian **plaquettes** of the Renaissance. On the east side is a display of European jewellery which includes four **pendants** with baroque pearls mounted as a dove, a rabbit, a dog, and a pelican (XII A61, 78, 82, 81), the first three being sixteenth-century German and the last eighteenth-century Mexican. The rare English sixteenth-century **hat-badge** (XII A62) is enamelled with *Judith and the head of Holofernes*. The north compartment shows the silver **hunting-collar** (III J508) of a Netherlandish archers' guild; the various shields record successive wearers from 1499 to 1826, while the collar itself dates from the fifteenth century. On the west side there is on the left a miscellany of European metal-work and to the right a selection of French royal portrait medallions which includes **Louis XII** (S153), a high relief in bronze of *c*.1500, and two bronze medals of **Henri IV and Marie de Médicis** (S369, S370) by Guillaume Dupré.

The visitor leaves the gallery by the corridor to the left of the back stairs (which lead up to Gallery 18) to enter the Back Corridor.

Back Corridor

The double swing-doors each side of the north entrance, installed in 1900, were resited in 1978. For further historical notes, see Galleries 5, 6 and 7.

Along the back corridor are six wall-cases. To the right, at the east end, case A contains lead-glazed **earthenwares** decorated with an incised white slip. Cases B to E show Italian **maiolica**; in B and C are further examples from Urbino, D

Drug Pot Tuscan maiolica (C81)

shows pieces from Faenza, Florence and Siena, and E examples from Cafaggiolo, Castel Durante, Fabriano and Venice. Case F at the west end contains a miscellany of eighteenth-century works of art in precious metals, hard-stones and porcelain. Of special interest are the rock-crystal and gold **ewer and basin** (I A27) made in Paris between 1727 and 1732; **boxes** and a **tray** of tortoiseshell and gold (*piqué*) (XXIII A28, 28a, 36), and two hard-paste porcelain **figures** (XII L179–80) made at Doccia in Italy in the mid-eighteenth century.

The visitor should now turn back down the Back Corridor and enter the last door on the left-hand side to enter Gallery 5, the first of four devoted to arms and armour.

Ewer and Basin French (I A27)

Galleries 5, 6 and 7

Galleries 5, 6 and 7 were created in 1897–1900. Wallace had displayed his European armoury in Gallery 20. Gallery 5 was the Coach House with a pantry and accommodation for the Grooms on a mezzanine floor above. Gallery 6 was stabling with a Grooms' mess-room above. Gallery 7 was also stabling with Grooms' rooms on a mezzanine floor above. There was originally a stable yard at the north entrance occupying a third of the north face. In 1900 Galleries 5 and 6 contained coupled free-standing columns at the west and east ends respectively; they were removed in 1920.

Galleries 5, 6 and 7 contain the magnificent collection of European arms and armour brought together by Sir Richard Wallace in 1871 (see p. 10). It is among the most important collections of its kind in the world, outside the great dynastic armouries of Vienna, Madrid, Paris and the Tower of London. The two main strengths of the collection are the number of finely decorated pieces of armour for parade, tournament and use in the field, and the series of sixteenth and seventeenth-century swords.

The arrangement is roughly chronological, but the visitor wishing to obtain the clearest history of the armourer's craft should visit Galleries 5 to 7 in reverse order. Very approximately Gallery 7 contains Medieval and Early Renaissance pieces mainly from the late-fourteenth to the early-sixteenth centuries; Gallery 6 High Renaissance examples from the sixteenth century, and Gallery 5 later pieces and all the firearms in the Collection. There is a separate Guide to the Wallace Collection Armouries.

Gallery 6 is to the right of the Back Corridor at the west side. Gallery 7 is to the left of the Back Corridor on the west side of the house. Gallery 8 is beyond it to the south.

Gallery 8

Gallery 8 was created in 1897–1900. Wallace had displayed his Oriental armoury in Gallery 16. Before 1900 this area contained, on the ground floor, an entrance lobby, the Butler's bed-room and sitting-room and a large stairwell leading down to the basement; on a mezzanine floor above were rooms for the Cook and the Lady's Maid. Until 1937, when the Oriental armoury was introduced from Gallery 4, this Gallery contained French sixteenth and seventeenth-century art. A door leading to the corridor between Galleries 10 and 11 was made in 1897–1900 and filled in during 1937.

This Gallery contains a part of the collection of Oriental arms and armour formed mainly by the 4th Marquess of Hertford in the last decade of his life, 1860–70. Such exotic armouries, as well as the Oriental subjects adopted by French nineteenth-century painters (also well represented here), were symptoms of the increasing impact of eastern art on western Europe, particularly as a consequence of Napoleon's Egyptian campaigns and the French colonisation of Algeria which began in 1830. The Wallace Collection's Oriental armoury was assembled mainly for its decorative effect (the Entrance Hall trophy shows the manner in which it was originally displayed) and neglects the earlier and simple forms of Oriental weaponry. There is a separate Guide to the Wallace Collection Armouries.

On the east wall hang a number of French nineteenth-century paintings of Oriental subjects. **Horace Vernet** travelled in Algeria in 1837 and 1853; **Decamps** repeatedly visited Turkey and the Middle East from *c.*1830, and **Marilhat** was in Egypt between 1831 and 1833.

The visitor leaves by the south door and enters Gallery 9.

Gallery 9

Landseer The Arab Tent
(P376) detail

Originally the Housekeeper's room with stairs leading down to the basement, and a workroom on a mezzanine floor above. Between 1900 and 1921 it was used exclusively as a Board room. In 1921 the doorways from Gallery 8 were introduced and portraits of the Founders were exhibited. In 1976 the sales-counter was introduced. The chandelier was installed in 1978.

Several nineteenth-century English pictures hang in this room, including the **Arab Tent** (P376), purchased by Wallace from the Prince of Wales, and **Looking for crumbs from the rich man's table** (P257), both by **Landseer.**

Gallery 10

Delacroix The Execution of
Marino Faliero (P282) detail

Originally the Breakfast Room with an additional door in the north wall leading to the service stairs; it was filled in during 1900. Between 1900 and 1978 the corridor leading to Gallery 11 had a higher, arched ceiling.

This Gallery is dominated by the paintings of **Richard Parkes Bonington** (1802–28), an Englishman whose short working life was centred on Paris, and **Eugène Delacroix** (1798–1863). For a few months in 1825 they travelled together in London and shared a studio in Paris. The pictures here reflect their common love of literary and historical subjects. On the east wall is Delacroix's imposing and original **Execution of the Doge Marino Faliero** (P282), the subject taken from an historical tragedy by Byron, and next to it hangs one of his illustrations to Goethe's **Faust** (P324). Bonington's histories are best represented by **Henri III receiving the Spanish Ambassador** (P323) and **François I and Marguerite of Navarre** (P322), both of which have a rich anecdotal quality. Bonington is at present better remem-

Bonington **Henri III** (P323)

beìed for his landscapes of which there are some outstanding examples, such as the early **Sea Piece** (P273) and the very fine **Coast Scene** (P341). The large view of the **Piazza S. Marco, Venice** (P375) was left unfinished at Bonington's death.

The remaining paintings in the gallery suggest Bonington's influence and include a little landscape by **Clarkson Stanfield** of **Orford**, a Hertford family borough (P354), works by **Eugène Isabey** (P271, P579), and history-pieces by **Paul Delaroche** such as the reduced but autograph version of his **Princes in the Tower** (P276), the original of which is in the Louvre.

The furniture includes the early-eighteenth-century boulle cupboard with **medal-cabinet and clock** (F413), which belonged to the 3rd Marquess of Hertford. There are four **high-backed chairs**: they are French nineteenth century (F463–6) in the style of the seventeenth century.

The visitor leaves the Gallery through a top-lit corridor in which a number of water-colours by **Bonington** and **J. M. W. Turner** are displayed. Outstanding amongst the many Boningtons are the **Leaning Towers, Bologna** (P701), the view of **Rouen** (P704), the **Interior of Sant 'Ambrogio, Milan** (P714)

33

and the magnificent **Sunset in the Pays de Caux** (P708) which reflects much sympathy with the work of his English contemporary, Turner. Four of Turner's water-colours of Yorkshire subjects, purchased by the 4th Marquess of Hertford in 1863, are shown here.

The visitor passes through the corridor into Gallery 11.

Bonington **Pays de Caux** (P708)

Gallery 11

Originally the Billiard Room with additional doors in the west and south walls leading to a cloakroom and service stairs respectively; they were filled in during 1900.

This Gallery contains fine boulle furniture, paintings and sculpture of the Louis XIV and Régence periods.

On the west wall above the chimney-piece hangs the well-known painting of **Louis XIV and his Heirs** (P122) attributed to **François de Troy**; the King, who reigned for seventy-two years, was eventually succeeded by his great-grandson (Louis XV), the little boy held on leading-strings by his Governess who probably commissioned this picture. On the chimneypiece below stand two **equestrian groups** (S191, S192) of gilt-bronze; they are reductions of the celebrated

F. de Troy (attributed) **Louis XIV and his Heirs** (P122) detail

Chevaux de Marly, the marble originals of which were made by G. Coustou the elder for the park of the Château de Marly; they now stand at the entrance to the Champs Elysées in Paris. At each end of the chimney wall stand fine works by **Antoine Coysevox**; on the left the bronze bust of **Louis XIV** (S165) of *c*.1699, and on the right the terracotta bust of **Charles Le Brun** (S60), the director of Louis XIV's Academy of Fine Arts, which Coysevox submitted to that Academy in 1676; in

Coysevox **Charles Le Brun** (S60)

35

1679 he completed a marble version which is now in the Louvre.

To the left and right of the chimney-piece hang large history pieces by **François Lemoyne** who was briefly the teacher of Boucher; just after he completed **Time revealing Truth** (P392) he committed suicide, an awful commentary on his subject.

On the facing east wall hangs the fine early-nineteenth-century wall-mirror with two **candelabra** (F51) in the manner of **A.-C. Boulle.** Below it stands the ornate **cabinet** (F16) veneered with floral marquetry and with terminal figures of carved pine-wood; it is probably in part by **Boulle** himself. In the centre of the gallery, standing on the boulle **writing-table** (F59), is the beautiful **toilet-mirror** (F50) also attributed to **Boulle** and bearing the arms of Charlotte de Saint-Simon, daughter of the famous diarist and courtier. Between the windows stands the large **wardrobe** (F61) from the Boulle workshop, similar to one in Gallery 2 (F62).

Against the south wall stands a nineteenth-century copy (F461) of a **desk** made by the Boulle workshop c.1715 for Maximilian Emanuel, Elector of Bavaria, and now in the Louvre. This copy was commissioned by the 4th Marquess of Hertford who substituted his own arms for those of the Elector.

The visitor passes through the east door to Gallery 12.

Gallery 12

Originally the Dining Room with additional doors in the alcoves leading back to the Entrance Hall; they were filled in during 1900. The cut-glass chandelier was introduced in 1978.

This Gallery shows eighteenth-century French decorative art, including a fine selection of Sèvres porcelain and gold boxes.

Carlin Table à pupitre
(F327)

The paintings include two masterpieces by J.-B. Oudry, the **Dead Roe** (P630) and the **Dead Wolf** (P626), both signed and dated 1721. On the north wall between the windows hang **A Hunt Breakfast** (P463) and the **Death of a Stag** (P470) by J.-F. de Troy; these lively sketches which are signed and dated 1737 were made for the larger pictures commissioned by Louis XV for his palace at Fontainebleau. Mlle de Clermont at her bath (P456) by J.-M. Nattier, dated 1733, suggests an exotic luxury in keeping with the sitter's eventful and romantic life, and the mood is maintained by the **Grand Turk giving a concert to his Mistress** (P451) by C.-A. Van Loo dated 1737.

Against the central window embrasure stands a **vase clock and candelabrum** (F272), of carrara marble and bronze, gilt and patinated; the winged bronze figure is perhaps after Falconet, and the whole dates from the second half of the eighteenth century. On either side of it are delicate Sèvresplaqued **work-tables** and **secretaires**; F304 is veneered with tulip-wood and purple-wood and the beautiful **table à pupitre** (F327) with tulip-wood; both are by **Martin Carlin**.

The furniture otherwise includes two **chests of drawers** (*commodes*) by or attributed to J.-H. **Riesener** (F248, F249) veneered with mahogany and with fine gilt-bronze mounts. On the north wall are set four very fine **wall-lights** (F366–9) made for the palace of Compiègne in 1787. The nineteenth-century French **pier-glass** (F439) was introduced in 1982.

In the centre of the Gallery stands a nineteenth-century copy (F460) of *le bureau du Roi,* the magnificent **roll-top desk** made by J.-F. Oeben and Riesener for Louis XV, completed in 1769 and now at Versailles. The copy, like the Elector's desk in Gallery 11, was commissioned by the 4th Marquess of Hertford.

Behind it stands a **table** mounted with Sèvres plaques (F316) supporting a glass show case in which is displayed a collection of French gold **snuff-boxes** made in Paris in the mid-eighteenth century. They echo in style and decoration the Sèvres porcelain also in this room. Painted enamels after Boucher are well represented and one made in 1749–50 (G8)

Gold Box Paris (G8)

shows translucent blue enamel scenes after his chinoiserie drawings. Other techniques of decoration include four-colour gold (G22, G27, G33), oriental lacquer (G40, G55, G60), tortoise-shell and gold *piqué* (G41, G66), and gouache miniatures by the **Van Blarenberghe** family (G36, G62).

In the wall cases on each side of the chimney-piece is a selection of Sèvres porcelain garnitures and tea-services which ranges in date from 1756–81 and includes fine examples of the rococo and neo-classical shapes and decorations for which the factory is so famous.

Wall-case A to the left contains three **vases** and a **tea-service** which may have belonged to Mme de Pompadour (IV

Garniture of three Vases Sèvres porcelain (IV B157–9)

Wine-cooler
from the Catherine II Service,
Sèvres porcelain (XX–XXI 6)

B142, 145, 162; XII B117), a **garniture** made for Louis XV (IV B157–9) and one bought by Marie-Antoinette in 1782 (IV A24–6). Also in this case are three **vases** (XII C153, 150–1) which were displayed as a garniture in the 4th Marquess of Hertford's bed-chamber at Hertford House.

To the right, wall-case B contains three **vases** with scenes after Boucher (XX–XXI 10–12); one is painted with the *Autumn Pastoral*, derived from his painting which hangs on the Landing (P482). There are also three of the famous turquoise-blue **ice and wine-coolers** from the service made for Catherine II of Russia in 1778–9 (XX–XXI 8–9, 13) and a hard-paste porcelain **tea service** dated 1779 (XII L165–6) decorated with unusual chinoiserie battle scenes.

The visitor should now return to the Entrance Hall and ascend the Grand Staircase.

Grand Staircase

The staircase is flanked by a magnificent **balustrade** (F68) of forged iron and bronze, chased and gilt; it was made between 1733 and 1741 for the *grand escalier d'honneur* leading to the King's Library in the old Palais Mazarin, now the Bibliothèque Nationale in Paris. It bears as part of the decoration the royal monogram of interlaced L's, sunflowers emblematic of the French kings, and cornucopias from which coins and medals emerge. It was sold as scrap-iron when the Palais Mazarin was reconstructed between 1855 and 1862, but is now considered the finest example of French iron and bronze work of this date to have survived. It was installed in Hertford House in 1872–5.

The staircase walls are hung with outstanding paintings by **François Boucher.** Facing the first flight of stairs are the

Balustrade French (F68) detail

Boucher The Rising of the Sun (P485) detail

Rising and the **Setting of the Sun** (P485, P486) dated respectively, 1753 and 1752; they were conceived as designs for Gobelins tapestries and once belonged to Mme de Pompadour, Boucher's most discerning patron. They are his most ambitious works, and he is said to have considered them his greatest achievement. On the side walls hang earlier works, the **Rape of Europa** (P484) and **Mercury confiding the infant Bacchus to the Nymphs** (P487); they were amongst the earliest purchases made by the 4th Marquess of Hertford and were once believed to be by François Lemoyne (see Gallery 11).

Landing

This is also hung with paintings by **Boucher,** including the large and very fine **Autumn** and **Summer Pastorals** (P482, P489) painted in 1749. The design for autumn is repeated on a Sèvres vase in Gallery 12. The two overdoors **Spring** (P445) and **Autumn** (P447) are dated 1745.

In the centre of the Landing is an engaging marble group of **Cupid and Psyche** (S22) inscribed **Cayot** and dated 1706.

On each side of the entrance to the Conservatory are two framed panels of **Gobelins tapestry** (F340, F341) by **P.-F. Cozette** after paintings by F.-H. Drouais. Beneath these are two fine **ewers** (F103, F104) of Meissen porcelain with gilt-bronze mounts attributed to **J. Caffiéri**, dateable 1745-9.

The visitor now passes through the left-hand doorway to enter Gallery 13.

Gallery 13

Originally the Small Drawing Room with an additional door on the west side leading back to the Landing; this was filled in during 1900. The north dividing wall was taken down at the same time and replaced with two free-standing fluted columns. The wall was put back in 1976.

This Gallery contains a number of fine paintings by Canaletto and Guardi. On the west wall hangs a set of four important Venetian views by **Guardi** showing **San Giorgio Maggiore** (P491), **The Dogana** (P494), **Santa Maria della Salute** (P503) and **The Rialto** (P508); they are among his finest

F. Guardi The Dogana, Venice (P494) detail

Canaletto **The Bacino, Venice** (P497) detail

Cressent **Cartel Clock** (F92)

works. Smaller views of the **Dogana** (P518) and **San Giorgio Maggiore** (P517) by the same artist are on the east wall to the left of the fireplace. His two architectural **caprices** (P502, P504) are by the windows, and a third (P647) is to the right of the fireplace. On the north wall hang two large and outstanding views by **Canaletto** of the **Bacino di San Marco** (P497, P499). To the left of the fireplace hang a pair of views of the Grand Canal (P506, P510) also by **Canaletto**.

The French furniture of the Louis XV period includes a fine **cabinet** (F70) and **chest of drawers** (F88) by **N.-J. Marchand**; the former is one of a pair made for Louis XV in 1755, the latter, veneered with lacquer, one of a pair made in the same year for his Queen, Marie Leczinska. On the south wall between the windows hangs the very fine **cartel clock** (F92); the gilt-bronze case made by **Charles Cressent** *c.*1750 incorporates the figures of *Love triumphing over Time*. Underneath it stands a fine **cartonnier** (F72) surmounted by a clock, made by **Charles Cressent**, but subsequently modified. On the eighteenth-century French **chimney-piece** (F251) stand a pair of Chinese celadon porcelain **vases** (F105, F106) mounted with French gilt-bronze between 1745–9, while a larger **vase** (F113) with similar mounts stands between them.

The visitor passes through the north doorway to enter Gallery 14.

Gallery 14

Originally the Large Drawing Room with an additional door on the east side leading to Gallery 16; this was filled in during 1937.

Fortier and Stollewerck
Régulateur Clock (F98) detail

This Gallery contains important collections of late boulle furniture and Sèvres porcelain. Among the paintings are more examples of **Canaletto**, including the carnival scenes **Fête on the Piazzetta** (P500) and **Regatta on the Grand Canal** (P496), and views of the north end of the **Grand Canal** (P507) and the **Rialto** (P511). Above the chimneypiece hangs a late-nineteenth-century view of **Venice** by **Félix Ziem** (P366), and a fine **Storm with Shipwreck** (P135) by **C.-J. Vernet**, dated 1754, is on the south wall.

Against the west wall stands the **Londonderry library-cabinet** (F390) made by **E. Levasseur** and once in the collection of the 3rd Marquess of Londonderry. It contains some Sèvres porcelain and four late-eighteenth-century Sèvres **vases** (XII 40–3) stand on it. On the wall above are four Louis XV gilt-bronze **wall-lights** (F119–22) in the style of **J. Caffiéri**. The very fine nine-light gilt-bronze **chandelier** (F84) hanging

43

Vase Sèvres porcelain (XX7)
detail

in the centre of the room is by **Caffiéri** himself and is probably contemporary with that in Gallery 2.

Between the windows on the north wall stands a remarkable **régulateur clock** (F98) with elaborate astronomical movements; it was made by **A. Fortier** and **M. Stollewerck**, with gilt-bronze mounts attributed to **J.-C. Duplessis** *père*, and once belonged to the banker Jean-Paris de Monmartel, god-father to Mme de Pompadour. On the chimney-piece stands a fine Louis XV **musical clock** (F96) by **C. Daillé** and **Stollewerck**, the case in the manner of **Duplessis** *père*. The late-eighteenth-century boulle **corner-cupboards** (F414, F415) in the south corners support a fine **clock and barometer** (F94, F95) veneered with lapis lazuli.

In the centre of the Gallery stand two cases containing Sèvres porcelain. Case 1 on the east side facing the fireplace shows pieces decorated with the dark blue ground colours, including the underglaze blue of Vincennes on **tea wares** with simple gilded decoration dated 1753 (IV A33–5), and the later overglaze blue, introduced in 1763, on a number of large **vases** painted with military and marine subjects and on a pair gilded with scenes of monkeys (XX 7–8).

Inkstand Sèvres porcelain
(XII B134)

Case 2 on the west side contains pieces with the green and rose grounds introduced in 1756 and 1757. The green-ground **inkstand** (XII B134) is dated 1758 and was probably made for Louis XV's daughter, Madame Adélaïde; the crown once contained a bell, the terrestrial globe is the inkwell and the celestial globe was probably for sand, shaken from the pierced stars to dry the ink. The rose-ground **flower vase** in the shape of a boat with lion masks at either end (XII C154) is dated 1757; the white reserve is painted with the interlaced L's of the French crown, which suggests it may have belonged to Louis XV or one of his family.

The visitor now turns back through Gallery 13 and turns left to enter Gallery 15.

Gallery 15

Originally the East Drawing Room with a central north door, added to Manchester House by the 2nd Marquess of Hertford by 1807. There appears to have been no fireplace before the nineteenth-century English chimney-piece, formerly in Gallery 3, was introduced in 1979. The north doorway was moved to the east side in 1979 to permit the construction of an emergency staircase to the second floor.

This Gallery contains Dutch and Flemish seventeenth-century paintings, including life-size half-length portraits by **Jacob Backer** (P89), **Ferdinand Bol** (P74, P78), **Willem Drost** (P61) and **Govaert Flinck** (P238) and two flower pieces by **Jan van Huijsum** (P149, P207) dating from the early-eighteenth century.

The furniture includes a fine Louis XIV boulle **console table** (F56) with a marquetry top showing monkeys walking the tightrope; there are also a pair of boulle **pedestal cabinets** (F395, F396), with medallions showing nymphs and satyrs, in the manner of **Adam Weisweiler**.

Boulle console table (P56) detail

The visitor passes through the north doorway to enter Gallery 16. In the short corridor a changing selection of old-master drawings is displayed on the east wall.

Gallery 16

Built by Ambler in 1872–5 for Wallace's Oriental armoury with a door at the north end of the west wall leading to Gallery 14, filled in during 1937. A flat glass lay-light was let into the coved ceiling in 1900; a pitched lay-light was introduced in 1920. The present ceiling was constructed in 1979–80.

This Gallery contains outstanding Dutch and Flemish seventeenth-century paintings.

Rembrandt The Good Samaritan
(P203)

Rubens The Marriage
of Henri IV (P521)

In the centre of the west wall is a group of magnificent oil
sketches by **Rubens**. Three (P522–4) dating from 1628–31 are
preparatory for a series of paintings commemorating the life
of Henri IV, commissioned by his Queen, Marie de Médicis,
for the Palais du Luxembourg but never completed. The
Defeat and Death of Maxentius (P520) is one of a series of
tapestry designs painted in 1621–2 illustrating the history of
the Emperor Constantine. To the left and right hang fine
sketches of the **Adoration of the Magi**. The one on the right
(P519) was made for an altarpiece commissioned in 1624 for
the Abbaye S. Michel and now in the Antwerp museum; the
one on the left (P521) was for an altarpiece commissioned in
1634 for the Convent of the White Sisters at Louvain, now in
the Chapel of King's College, Cambridge. On either side
hang works by **David Teniers**, while above are fine landscapes by **Meindert Hobbema** (P60), **Jan Wijnants** (P160, P190)
and **Jacob van Ruisdael** (P156). Either side of the north door
hang domestic interiors by **Nicolaes Maes**, the **Listening
Maid** (P224) dated 1656 and the **Housewife at work** (P239).

ter Borch **Lady reading a letter** (P236)

In the centre of the east wall hang two paintings by **Rembrandt**, a **Self-portrait** of 1634 (P52), and the **Landscape with a Coach** (P229) of 1637; the **Good Samaritan** (P203) was until recently attributed to him. Near the centre hang two pictures of hermits by **Rembrandt's** pupil, **Gerrit Dou** (P170, P177). At each end of the wall are fine genre pieces by **Gabriel Metsu**, including the **Letter Writer surprised** (P240) and the **Sleeping Sportsman** (P251). To the left is the very fine **Lady reading a Letter** (P236) by **Gerard ter Borch**. Above these genre pieces hang landscapes by **Aert van der Neer** and **Jacob van Ruisdael** whose **Rocky Landscape** (P50) hangs on the south wall, alongside **Merrymaking in a tavern** (P158) by **Jan Steen**.

The furniture in this Gallery includes a Louis XIV boulle **knee-hole writing-table**, with top veneered in the style of **Jean Berain** showing Apollo surrounded by grotesques and animals (F57). There are also two late-eighteenth-century boulle **side tables**; one with a top veneered with an oxcart design is by **René Dubois** (F424) and the other whose top shows an elaborate *singerie* is by **J.-F. Leleu** (F425).

The visitor passes through the north doorway to enter Gallery 17.

Rembrandt **Landscape with a Coach** (P229)

Gallery 17

Like Galleries 18 and 20, built by Ambler in 1872–5 as a picture gallery with a coved ceiling incorporating a flat lay-light. Pitched lay-lights were introduced in 1920, and the present lower ceilings were constructed in 1979–80.

This Gallery contains a collection of fine seventeenth-century Dutch paintings.

Hobbema A Watermill (P99)

In the centre of the west wall on the left is the lively **Christening Feast** (P111) painted in 1664 by **Jan Steen** whose charming **Harpsichord Lesson** (P154) and more robust **Lute Player** (P150) hang below. Beside them hang seascapes by **Willem van de Velde** (P221, P215), together with genre scenes by **Adriaen van Ostade** (P169, P202) and the attractive **Lace Maker** (P237) of 1664 by **Caspar Netscher**. On the top line hang three fine landscapes by Meindert Hobbema (P95, P99 and P164) with two more seascapes by van de Velde (P246, P194).

On the east wall are three little panels showing cattle scenes by **Paulus Potter** (P189, P252 and P219), and three meticulous townscapes by **Jan van der Heyden** (P225, P195 and P230).

Camphuijsen **A Dutch Farm at Sunset** (P132) detail

On the top line is the **Battle of Scheveningen** by **Willem van de Velde** (P77) and **Govert Camphuijsen**'s most accomplished landscape, the **Dutch Farm at Sunset** (P132).

Either side of the south door hang domestic interiors by **Pieter de Hoogh, A Woman peeling apples** (P23) and **A Boy bringing pomegranates** (P27), while on the north wall, either side of the doorway into Gallery 18, hang slightly later cabinet pictures by **Willem van Mieris** (P155 and P163) and **Adriaen van der Werff** (P151 and P165), the latter remarkable for their high degree of finish.

The furniture includes a Louis XIV boulle **knee-hole writing-table**, with a top inlaid with mother-of-pearl showing *Diana and Actaeon* (F58).

The visitor passes through the north door to Gallery 18.

Gallery 18

See note on Gallery 17. Galleries 17 and 18 were one, originally used by Wallace to display his nineteenth-century French paintings now in Gallery 20. In 1979 a dividing wall was introduced to create the two Galleries. The north wall was also modified in 1979 to contain heating ducts, resulting in the creation of the alcove over the back stairs.

This Gallery contains Dutch seventeenth-century paintings which may broadly be characterised as having been influenced by the art and landscape of Italy. The display may alter during the winter months to permit special exhibitions concerning aspects of the Collection.

In the centre of the west wall on the left is the powerful **Landscape with Animals** (P57) by **Adam Pynacker**. To the left and right of it hang **Aelbert Cuyp's** fine views of the **Ferry-boat on the Maas** (P54) and of the **Avenue at Meerdervoort** (P51), which shows Dordrecht in the distance. There are also paintings by **Philips Wouwermans**, including his lyrical **By the Riverside** (P226), and **Nicholas Berchem**.

Cuyp **The Avenue at Meerdervoort** (P51)

In the centre of the east wall hangs **Shipping on the Maas** (P49) by **Cuyp**. It is flanked with port scenes by **Berchem**, the **Old Port of Genoa** (P25), and by **J. B. Weenix** (P117), whose son **Jan Weenix** painted many of the dead game pieces in the adjoining Gallery 19. At each end of the wall hang fine Italianate landscapes by **Jan Both** (P24, P28). On the south wall hangs the **Horse Fair** (P65), one of the most celebrated compositions of **Wouwermans**.

In the alcove over the stairs on the north wall is set an eighteenth-century copy (P5) of Titian's painting, *The Rape of Europa* (now in the Isabella Stewart Gardner Museum, Boston); the copy is placed here so that the visitor may see with it through the north door the **Perseus and Andromeda** (P11) by **Titian** in Gallery 19 which was once the companion of the original in the collections of Philip II of Spain and the duc d'Orléans in France.

The Gallery furniture includes a pair of veneered **corner-cupboards,** one (F100) stamped by **J. Dubois**, but evidently cut down from a larger piece of furniture, the other (F101) made to match by **A. Fleury**.

The visitor passes through the north door into Gallery 19. The staircase on the right leads down to Gallery 4.

Gallery 19

Built by Ambler in 1872–5. The coved ceiling originally had a flat glass lay-light spanning the Gallery. The present ceiling was introduced in 1981. The parquet border of the floor, taken up in 1900 when iron heating grilles were installed, was restored in 1981. The Gallery was occupied by the Intelligence division of the Admiralty during the first world war when temporary windows were made in the south wall.

Gallery 19 is one of the finest picture galleries in the world. It contains seventy paintings, the majority dating from 1620–70; Rembrandt, Velazquez, Rubens, Van Dyck, Titian, Poussin and Claude are superbly represented. Above the main line of pictures hang a number of seventeenth-century Dutch and Flemish still-life and hunting scenes, including fourteen by **Jan Weenix**.

Opposite the door on entering, on the north wall, is the **Perseus and Andromeda** (P11) by **Titian**, painted in 1554 for

Titian **Perseus and Andromeda** (P11)

Philip II of Spain, one of seven magnificent *poesie* (poetic subjects drawn from the works of Ovid) now dispersed in Madrid, Boston USA, Edinburgh and the National Gallery, London. This picture was cleaned and restored in 1978–82. To the left is the large and awesome **Landscape with Apollo and the Cumaean Sibyl** (P116) by **Salvator Rosa** which belonged to Cardinal Mazarin. To the left again is the **Dance to the music of Time** (P108) by **Poussin**, painted for Cardinal Rospigliosi (later Pope Clement IX) *c.*1638; it shows the figures of poverty, work, riches and pleasure treading the measure of life.

Poussin A Dance to the music of Time (P108) detail

Salvator Rosa Apollo and the Cumaean Sibyl (P116) detail

In the centre of the north wall are two splendid full-length portraits painted by **Van Dyck** in Antwerp of **Philippe le Roy** (P94) and his wife **Marie de Raet** (P79). They hang each side of the superb **Rainbow Landscape** (P63) by **Rubens**, painted from Het Steen, his country house near Brussels, in the closing years of his life; the picture was cleaned in 1982. It is a companion piece to the well-known *Château de Steen* in the National Gallery, London.

Continuing down the north wall there is the very fine **Landscape with Mercury stealing the flocks of Admetus from Apollo** (P114), painted by **Claude** in Rome in 1660. The

Rubens **The Rainbow Landscape** (P63) detail

Van Dyck **Philippe Le Roy** (P94)
detail

Velazquez **Lady with a fan** (P88)

subject is again taken from Ovid. Next to it hangs the magnificent Spanish portrait of a **Lady with a fan** (P88) by **Velazquez**, one of his few portraits not of a Court sitter. There follow four more Spanish pictures; the **Adoration of the Shepherds** (P34) and **Joseph and his Brethren** (P46) by **Murillo** which hung in a Capuchin Convent in Genoa between 1678 and 1805, together with the **Charity of S. Thomas of Villanueva** (P97) which hangs at the east end of the opposite wall; and two portraits of Prince Balthazar Carlos, the son of Philip IV of Spain who predeceased his father at the age of sixteen. One showing him in the riding school is probably by **Juan del Mazo**, Velazquez's pupil and son-in-law who was the Prince's Painter (P6), the other showing him in infancy is by Velazquez himself (P12).

On the west wall hang seven English portraits by Reynolds, Gainsborough, Lawrence and Romney. In the centre is **Lawrence's** informal yet imposing **George IV** (P559) painted in 1822. Forty years before as Prince of Wales he had fallen for Mrs Robinson of whom there are three portraits here; the poetical full-length by **Gainsborough** (P42) showing her holding a miniature with a pomeranian dog by her side, and heads by **Romney** (P37) and **Reynolds** (P45). There are also two very fine Reynolds, of the courtesan **Nelly O'Brien** (P38) painted in the 1760s, and of **Mrs Carnac** (P35) a full-length painted in 1775–6.

Gainsborough
Mrs Robinson (P42) detail

Turning to the south wall, **Christ's charge to Peter** (P93) by Rubens, hanging to the right of the doorway, once hung in the chapel of Ste. Gudule in Brussels. To the left of the doorway hang the **Falls of Tivoli** (P139), one of the best works by Poussin's brother-in-law, **Gaspard Dughet**, and Spanish pictures by **Murillo** (P68) and **Alonso Cano** (P15). The **Migration of Jacob** (P80) was painted in 1663 by **Adriaen van de Velde**, brother of **Willem van de Velde the younger** whose masterly **Dutch Man-o'-War saluting** (P137) hangs in the centre of the south wall (and who is well represented in Gallery 17). Between the brothers' works are other important Dutch pictures.

Hals The Laughing Cavalier (P84)

Reynolds Nelly O'Brien (P38) detail   Rembrandt Titus (P29)

The **Laughing Cavalier** (P84), perhaps the most famous picture in the Wallace Collection, is a masterpiece by **Frans Hals** painted in Haarlem in 1624 and given its slightly misleading title in London in the 1870s. Next to it is a fine **Stormy Landscape** (P75) by **Hobbema** dated 1663. Either side of the big sea-piece hang the sombre full-length portraits by **Rembrandt** of Jan Pellicorne, a merchant of Leiden, and his wife and children (P82, P90). To the left again is the ominous **Landscape with a waterfall** (P56) by **Ruisdael** and beyond it the beautiful yet melancholy portrait by **Rembrandt** of his son **Titus** (P29) painted *c.*1657; Titus died at the age of twenty-eight just before his father.

Beyond this group of Dutch pictures are further works by **Murillo** (P97, P58), and a fine three-quarter length portrait by **Van Dyck** of **Isabella Waerbeke** (P16). To the right of the doorway is the **Virgin and Child with S. John** (P9) by **Andrea del Sarto**, the finest version of a well-known composition. To the left of the doorway is **S. Catherine of Alexandria** (P1) by **Cima da Conegliano**, painted *c.*1500 for the church of S. Rocco in Mestre, near Venice.

57

On the east wall hang three outstanding works by **Philippe de Champaigne**: the **Adoration of the Shepherds** (P129), commissioned by Cardinal Richelieu in 1628; the huge **Annunciation** (P134) from the mid-1640s, and the frieze-like **Marriage of the Virgin** (P119) of the same period. The brilliantly coloured **Marriage of S. Catherine** (P646) by **Sassoferrato** completes the wall.

The furniture includes, at each end of the Gallery, a pair of eighteenth-century Italian **tables** (F514, F515) of *verde antico* marble mounted with pine-wood, carved and gilt. Down the centre of the Gallery are displayed a pair of seventeenth-century Italian **tables** (F510, F511) of carved lime-wood, with tops of stone veneered with red Egyptian porphyry. In the centre of the Gallery is a Louis XVI-style **writing-table** (F320) veneered with hazel-wood banded with rosewood and with gilt-bronze mounts. At the west end of the north wall is a **chest of drawers** (F405); it is in the style of Boulle and relates closely to one of Berain's engraved designs.

The bronze **groups** and **statuettes** displayed on the tables include versions of well-known models by **Giovanni da Bologna** (see also Gallery 3) and some fine seventeenth and eighteenth-century French bronzes.

The visitor leaves by the west door to enter Gallery 20.

Gallery 20

See note on Gallery 17. Used by Wallace as his European Armoury (which was moved to galleries 5, 6 and 7 in 1900). The north wall was modified in 1979 to contain heating ducts, resulting in the creation of the alcove on the west side over the back stairs.

Gallery 20 contains a rich collection of French nineteenth-century paintings from the period 1820–60, such as would have been seen in the official Salon exhibitions. The 4th Marquess of Hertford knew several of the artists, such as Meissonier, Decamps and Horace Vernet, and he also commissioned works directly, such as the pair of **flower-pieces** (P760, P761) by **Saint-Jean**, on the south wall, and the **Virgin and Child** (P286) by **Delaroche** on the east.

The west, right-hand, wall is dominated by the large **Paolo and Francesca** (P316), painted by **Ary Scheffer** in 1835, one of several versions of the subject; the frame, which further elaborates Dante's text, was probably devised by the artist. On the left are grouped a number of paintings by **Bellangé**, **Schopin**, **Gros** and **Horace Vernet** commemorating the exploits of Napoleon, their corporate purpose best exemplified in the **Apotheosis of Napoleon** (P575) painted by **Vernet** in the year of the exiled Emperor's death. Other works on this wall include, from the right, the large **Venus and Adonis** (P347) commissioned from **Prud'hon** by the Empress Marie-

Meissonier **An Artist showing his work** (P325)

Louise in 1810; **The Sleep of Venus and Cupid** (P348) by Prud'hon's pupil and confidante, **Marie-Françoise Mayer**, commissioned by the Empress Josephine (whose portrait by **Prud'hon** hangs in the alcove on the north wall), and **The Lion in Love** (P285) by **Roqueplan**, the subject taken from a fable by La Fontaine.

On the south wall are grouped a number of cabinet pictures by **Meissonier**, including **Polichinelle** (P337) which was painted on a door panel in the apartment of Mme Sabatier, the **Artist showing his work** (P325), the **Roadside Inn** (P328) and the charming **Young Poet** (P326) which was shown at the Salon in 1853.

In the centre of the east wall hangs **Margaret at the Well** (P284), from Goethe's *Faust*, by **Scheffer** dated 1858. On each side of it on the upper line are Barbizon landscapes by **Troyon** (P344) and **Théodore Rousseau** (P283), and two Biblical scenes in Oriental settings by **Vernet, Judah and Tamar** (P346) and **Joseph's Coat** (P349). Along the lower line hang a number of cabinet pictures by **Delaroche, Decamps, Diaz,** and **Eugène Isabey**.

On the north wall, to the right of the door, hang more cabinet pictures by **Thomas Couture** and **Delaroche**.

Against the west wall in the centre stands a **chest of drawers** veneered with mahogany (F246) made by **J.-F. Leleu** in 1772 for the Palais-Bourbon in Paris. Against the opposite wall in the centre stands the early-nineteenth-century boulle **writing-desk** (F479) made in London in the French style by **L. C. Le Gaigneur**.

In the centre of the Gallery are two upright covered cases (the visitor should lift the covers) containing a selection of early-nineteenth-century miniatures. Case 1 at the south end is devoted principally to Napoleonic subjects; there are portraits of the Emperor by **Isabey, Saint, Augustin** and **Muneret** ranging in date from *c.*1798 to 1815, with portraits of his brothers Louis and Jerome, and sisters Pauline and Caroline. There are portraits of the Empress Josephine by **Isabey** (R187), **Aubrey, Saint** and **Quaglia**, and of the Empress Marie-Louise by **Isabey** and **Menuisier**.

J.-B. Isabey
Napoleon I (R184)

J.-B. Isabey
Rose Maystre (R206)

Case 2 at the north end contains a selection of fine miniatures by **Augustin, Mansion** and **Isabey** whose portraits of himself (R178), the **Duke of Wellington** (R198), his wife, **Rose Maystre** (R206) and **Prince August of Prussia** (R193) are of particular interest. There is also a portrait of **Mme de Staël** (R163) by the Swiss **Arlaud-Jurine**.

The staircase at the north end leads down to Gallery 7, but the visitor should pass through the south door to Gallery 21.

Gallery 21

Originally three rooms built by Ambler in 1872–5: from the north Wallace's dressing-room and Lady Wallace's bath room and dressing room. Converted to a top-lit gallery in 1900, with an additional door on the east side leading to the corridor between Galleries 23 and 24: this was filled in during 1920. The ceiling has been modified as described for Gallery 16.

This Gallery contains perhaps the finest collection of French eighteenth-century painting and furniture to be seen in a single room. There are also miniatures dating from the sixteenth to the eighteenth centuries.

The pictures are by Watteau, his two followers Lancret

Watteau **Gilles and his Family** (P381)

61

Watteau **La Toilette** (P439)

and Pater, and by Boucher, Fragonard and Greuze. They
cover the whole of the eighteenth century.

The collection of paintings by **Watteau** is one of the most
extensive to be seen anywhere, and includes some of his finest
works. On the west wall are the two large and late works, the
Halt (P416) to the right, and the **Fête in a Park** (P391) to the left.
A reduced but superior version of the latter, **Les Champs
Elysées** (P389) hangs between them with other Watteaus. The
figure of the lutanist in the tiny **Music Lesson** (P377), recurs in
the celebrated **Music Party** (P410); one of the most beautiful of
all is the tiny **Gilles and his Family** (P381), a melancholy yet
charming picture wholly characteristic of the master. Such
commedia dell'Arte figures, derived from the itinerant Italian
actors playing out themes of dalliance and intrigue, recur in
the **Harlequin and Columbine** (P387). **La Toilette** (P439)
demonstrates Watteau's admiration for both Rubens and
Veronese.

Watteau's followers Lancret and Pater are also well represented. On the south wall the **Italian comedians by a Fountain** (P465) by **Lancret** is one of his most elaborate and successful pictures and the **Conversation galante** (P422) on the west wall was submitted to the *académie* as his diploma work in 1719. On the same wall his **Bird-Catchers** (P436) and **Mlle Camargo dancing** (P393) are noteworthy; Mlle Camargo was a Spanish dancer who made her debut in Paris in 1726. **Pater's** well-known **Vivandières de Brest** (P452) hangs on the east wall, together with his **Watching the Dance** (P380) and other *fêtes galantes*.

The works by **Boucher** comprise the charming interior scene **La Modiste** (P390) painted in 1746 and two overdoor pastorals on the east wall (P385, P399).

There is a very distinguished group of works by **Fragonard** covering twenty-five years of his working life. The earliest is the idyllic **Gardens of the Villa d'Este at Tivoli** (P379), and the most famous **The Swing** (P430), a curious subject commissioned in 1768–9 by the Baron de Saint-Julien who evaluates his mistress from a vantage point in the bushes; it is a succulent and delightful picture. The **Souvenir** (P382), the **Schoolmistress** (P404), and the **Young Scholar** (P455) are charming genre scenes from the 1770s. The **Fountain of Love** (P394), whose sombre mood and colouring is in such contrast to the gaiety of the **Swing**, dates from *c.*1785. Further works by **Fragonard** are shown in Galleries 23 and 25.

At the north end of the Gallery are seven paintings by **Greuze**, whose sentimental female heads particularly appealed to the 4th Marquess of Hertford. There are further works by **Greuze** in Galleries 23 and 25.

The furniture and *bronzes d'ameublement* (furnishing bronzes) in this Gallery are of great importance. The principal feature is a remarkable series of drop-front secretaires, a type of furniture which came into general use in France *c.*1750, but first the visitor should look at the earlier chests of

Fragonard **The Swing** (P430)

Gaudreau **Chest of Drawers** (F86)

drawers placed in the centre of the two long walls which are of special magnificence.

On the east side is one (F86) veneered with kingwood and mahogany and lavishly mounted with gilt-bronze in the full rococo manner; it was made by A.-R. Gaudreau in 1739 for the bedroom of Louis XV in the *appartement intérieur* at Versailles; the bronzes are signed by J. Caffiéri. Two fine gilt and silvered bronze rococo **candlesticks** after J.-A. **Meissonnier** stand on this chest of drawers. On the west side is another **chest of drawers** (F85) veneered with kingwood which has elaborate gilt-bronze mounts partly in the form of dragons; it was made by **Charles Cressent**, perhaps from designs by **N. Pineau**.

Perhaps the most imposing of the later **secretaires** is one at the north end of the east wall, made in 1780 by J.-H. Riesener for Marie-Antoinette's *petits appartements* at Versailles (F300). Opposite this stands another (F303) veneered with thuya-wood and made *en suite* with one of the **corner cupboards** (F275, F276) by **Riesener** in 1783 for Marie-Antoinette at Versailles, but transferred to Marly in the same year. The **secretaire** at the south end of the west wall (F302) was also made by **Riesener** in 1783 for the Queen at the Petit Trianon, Versail-

65

Cressent **Chest of Drawers** (F85) detail

Riesener **Secretaire** (F302) detail

les; the marquetry incorporates the water-lilies characteristic of **Riesener** and the plaque of the drop-front is in the manner of **Clodion**. Opposite it stands an example richly decorated with pictorial marquetry by **Foulet** and bearing the arms of the Comtes d'Hane-Steenhuyse of Ghent (F299). Between the doors on the south wall stands a **chest of drawers** (F247) with water-lily marquetry which was probably made by **Riesener** in 1780 for Marie-Antoinette at Versailles.

There are also a number of small tables of fine quality, including, on the east wall, the **combined work and toilet-table** (F110) attributed to **J.-F. Oeben** which has extensive interior fitments.

The *bronzes d'ameublement* include a number of fine **clocks**; one is in the form of a group representing *Love triumphing over Time* with the movement encased in a celestial globe (F264), and another resembles one made for Marie-Antoinette at Saint-Cloud (F263). A particularly good example has a case of two winged sphinxes supporting the clock on a cushion with two billing doves surmounting the face (F269).

The pair of gilt-bronze **candlesticks** (F164, F165) was made by **Pitoin** in 1781 for Marie-Antoinette at Versailles to celebrate the birth in that year of the Dauphin, whose title is symbolised by the dolphins on the bases.

Pitoin **Candlestick**
one of a pair (F165)

Mantel Clock French (F263)

François Clouet **Renée Baillet** (R2)

Horenbout
Hans Holbein (R3)

In the centre of the gallery are two covered hexagonal cases containing miniatures (the visitor should lift the covers). Case 1 at the south end shows English and Continental miniatures from the sixteenth to the mid-eighteenth centuries. On the south side are the earlier pieces. In the centre is the portrait of **Holbein** (R3) by **Lucas Horenbout**; it is flanked by **Jean de Thou** (R1) and his wife **Renée Baillet** (R2) by **François Clouet**. These are perhaps the most important miniatures in the collection. Other works on this side include portraits by **Samuel Cooper, Isaac Oliver,** and **John Hoskins**. On the west side is a rare miniature by **Rosalba Carriera** (R36) and several *galant* subjects by **Jacques Charlier** who was probably the pupil of Boucher. On the east side are late-eighteenth and nineteenth-century English miniatures which include **Mrs Fitzherbert** (R149) by **Cosway** and individual examples of **Engleheart, Smart** and **Mee**.

67

Case 2 at the north end shows, on the north side, several copies of portraits by Reynolds, Lely and Lawrence, including **Mrs Robinson** (R317) by **John Hazlitt**, brother of the well-known essayist, and the **Countess of Blessington** (R322) from the portrait hanging in Gallery 1. On the south side is an important collection of French miniatures from the same period. There is an outstanding group by **Peter Adolf Hall** including his **Family** (R107) and daughter **Adélaïde-Victorine** (R108). Two miniatures are attributed to **Fragonard** (R91, R92). There are four *galant* subjects by **Niclas Lafrensen** (R94–7) and a charming portrait of **Georgiana, Duchess of Devonshire** with her friend **Lady Elizabeth Foster** (R137) by **J.-U. Guérin**. The full-length of **Marguerite Gérard**, the pupil of Fragonard (R134) is by **François Dumont** (an identification made since the Catalogue of Miniatures was published in 1980). In the north-east section is a portrait of Louis XVI's son (R135), who died in captivity at the age of ten, by the same artist.

The visitor leaves through either of the south doors to enter Gallery 22.

Hall
The Artist's Family (R107)

Gallery 22

Formerly Lady Wallace's bedroom; added to Manchester House by the 2nd Marquess of Hertford by 1807.

This Gallery is dominated by the work of **Boucher**. On the east and west walls are shown a set of four decorative panels painted in 1754: **Venus and Vulcan** (P429), **Venus and Mars** (P438), **Cupid a captive** (P432) and the **Judgment of Paris** (P444). In the centre of the east wall hangs the very fine portrait of **Mme de Pompadour** (P418) painted in 1759; opposite it is the large oval **Jove in the shape of Diana surprises Calisto** (P446).

Over the late-eighteenth-century **chimney-piece** (F250) is a good version of **L.-M. van Loo**'s state portrait of **Louis XV**

Boizot, Gouthière and Delunésy The Avignon
Clock (F258)

(P177), the original of which was painted in 1761. Below it
stands the very fine **mantel clock** (F258) made by **Gouthière**
after a design by the sculptor **L.-S. Boizot**; it was a gift from
the City of Avignon in 1771 to Jean-Louis-Roger, marquis de
Rochechouart, who had taken the City back from Papal
authority in 1768.

Against the centre of the west wall stands the very fine
lacquer **chest of drawers** (F245) by **R. Dubois,** supporting the
red jasper **perfume-burner** (F292) with exquisite gilt-bronze
mounts by **P. Gouthière.** The pair of **tables** (F317, F318) on
either side, of cast-iron exquisitely mounted with gilt-bronze,
are in the manner of **A. Weisweiler,** but the mounts have
been attributed to **P. Gouthière.** In the centre of the room is
the fine **writing-table** (F112) dating from the mid-eighteenth

R. Dubois **Chest of Drawers** (F245) detail

Gouthière
Perfume-burner (F292)

century veneered on oak with tulip-wood and kingwood and mounted lavishly with gilt-bronze.

The visitor leaves by the east door to enter Gallery 23.

Gallery 23

Formerly Lady Wallace's boudoir with an additional door in the north wall leading to the service stairs, filled in during 1900. The existing arch leading to the corridor was formed in 1900 and replaced a standard door-frame.

This Gallery contains a collection of late-eighteenth-century English and French sentimental and moral genre pieces illustrating the cult of *sensibilité* otherwise seen in the contemporary writings of Rousseau and Diderot.

On the north wall hang two of **Reynolds**'s most popular studies of children, **Miss Bowles** (P36) and the **Strawberry**

Greuze **The Broken Mirror** (P442)

R. Dubois **Cartonnier** (F178) detail

Girl (P40) from the period 1773–5. Between them is **Inno-cence** by **Greuze** (P384), an immensely popular picture in the later-nineteenth century; it is flanked by two scenes painted by the same artist in the early 1760s, the **Inconsolable Widow** (P454), also known as *le tendre ressouvenir*, and the **Broken Mirror** (P442), *le malheur imprévu*, which illustrate the themes of grief and slovenliness.

On the east wall hang three works by **Boilly** painted in 1789–90 (P435, P473, P479) which define some of the hazards of female sensibility, together with **The Visit to the Boarding School** by **Morland** (P574), also painted *c.*1789. On the south wall the **Musical Contest** by **Fragonard** (P471), an early work showing the influence of Boucher, hangs between the windows.

The furniture includes the outstanding *ensemble* consisting of **writing-table, inkstand and cartonnier** (F330, F287, F178) by **R. Dubois**, of oak lacquered with green *vernis Martin*, made *c.*1763 possibly for Catherine II of Russia. The small **work table** (F325) by **A. Weisweiler** against the north wall was at one time in the Empress Josephine's apartments in the Tuileries, and the **toilet table** (F321) is attributed to **B. Moli-**

71

tor. On the grey-marble Louis XVI **chimney-piece** (F252) is a
fine gilt-bronze **mantel clock** (F266), also of the Louis XVI
period, flanked by **candelabra** (F140–1) with bronze figures of
Cupid and Psyche after **Falconet**. To the right of the chimney-piece stands the **secretaire** (F301) by **J.-F. Leleu**, veneered
on oak with pictorial marquetry.

The visitor passes through the north doorway to enter
Gallery 24 via a corridor. On the right a wall-case contains a
travelling service of silver-gilt, intended for toilet, writing
and eating, and consisting of fifty-seven pieces; it is German,
and was made at Augsburg in 1767–73. On the left is the very
rare **perpetual almanac** (F64–7) in four parts, of enamel on
copper framed with gilt-bronze, by **A.-N. Martinière** 1741–
2; each part contains enamel slips with chronological data,
Saints' days and the signs of the Zodiac.

Canteen silver-gilt, Augsburg

Martinière Perpetual Almanac (F64)

Gallery 24

Formerly Wallace's study, with an additional door in the south wall leading to the service stairs filled in during 1900. The existing arch leading to the corridor was formed in 1900, and replaced a standard door-frame.

This Gallery contains fine boulle furniture and decorative panels by the *animaliers* A.-F. Desportes and J.-B. Oudry. Those by **Desportes** on the west wall (P594, P628) were painted in 1715; the set of four by **Oudry** (P625, P627, P629, P631) were

Musical clock (F97)

Pedestal Clock (F42) detail

painted for the financier J.-C. Trudaine and shown at the Salon of 1748.

On the chimney-piece stands the **musical clock** (F97) with a finely cast and chased gilt-bronze case. The **pier-glass** (F444) is of nineteenth-century French workmanship.

At the east end of the north wall stands a **long-case clock** (F271) with a case veneered with ebony in a severely classical style by **B. Lieutaud**; its movement, by **F. Berthoud**, has a compensating pendulum of alternate strips of steel and brass.

In the centre of the south wall is a particularly fine **pedestal clock** (F42), probably from the Boulle workshop, mounted with gilt-bronze figures representing the four continents of Europe, Asia, Africa and America.

The **sofas** and **armchairs** (F185–92) are of the Louis XVI period, but are covered with Louis XV Beauvais tapestry covers, made to designs by **J.-B. Oudry**.

The visitor passes through the east doorway to enter Gallery 25.

Gallery 25

Originally the Oval Drawing Room; it is the only room to retain its original fire-place, the decoration of which echoes that in the ceiling frieze above. The cut-glass chandelier was introduced in 1980.

This Gallery contains outstanding pieces of later-eighteenth-century French furniture and sculpture, a fine collection of gold boxes and a number of later-eighteenth-century French paintings.

Over the chimney-piece hangs the **Votive offering to Cupid** (P441) by **Greuze**, shown at the Salon of 1769 when Diderot was quick to criticise the drawing of the figure. On each side of it are late-eighteenth-century French portraits: the so-called **Sophie Arnould** (P403), which used to hang by

Greuze Sophie Arnould (P403)

Houdon Madame de Sérilly (S26)

Felois Wall-light
from a set of four (F374)

Lord Hertford's bed in the rue Laffitte, and the **Girl with Doves** by **Greuze** (P428); **Mme Perregaux** (P457) and the **Comte d'Espagnac** (P449) by **Mme Vigée Lebrun**, and **Boy as Pierrot** (P412) by **Fragonard**, thought to show the artist's son.

Round the north wall hang two portraits by **Nattier** of **Mlle de Chateaurenaud** (P461) dated 1755 and the **comtesse de Tillières** (P453) dated 1750. Between them stand two magnificent busts in white marble by **Jean-Antoine Houdon**: the formidable **Madame Victoire of France** (S25), fifth daughter of Louis XV, dated 1777, and the serene **Mme de Sérilly** (S26) dated 1782.

On the chimney-piece stands a fine **mantel clock** (F268) of gilt and patinated bronze with figures of *Night* and *Day* after Michelangelo; and on the wall are four gilt-bronze **wall-lights** (F374–7) of exceptional quality made in 1787 by **L.-G. Felois** and others for the use of Marie-Antoinette at the château de Saint-Cloud. Against this wall stands an important set of six chairs (F233–8) made in 1786 by **J.-B. Boulard** and others for Louis XVI's card-room at Fontainebleau;

75

Riesener Roll-top Desk (F102)

they were re-upholstered in 1982 to imitate their original blue and white *lampas*.

Against the central window embrasure stands a large vase of white marble carved with reliefs (S32), signed by **Claude Michel**, called **Clodion**.

Next to it is the magnificent **roll-top desk** (F102) made in 1769 by **Riesener**. It is veneered on oak with a marquetry of great richness and is mounted with bronze, chased and gilt. In the marquetry on the sides is a monogram, recently identified by the French scholar Christian Baulez as that of Pierre Grimod, comte d'Orsay (1748–1809), for whose hôtel d'Orsay in the rue de Varenne this desk was presumably made. It is similar in style to the famous *bureau du Roi* at Versailles of which there is a copy (F460) in Gallery 12.

Beyond the desk is a nineteenth-century carved **gilt table** supporting a glass case in which a number of gold **snuff-boxes** are displayed. They are decorated with enamels and hardstones and were made in Paris, Vienna, Geneva and Dresden in the eighteenth century. The French boxes include some with enamel portraits of Louis XIV and members of his court by, or in the style of **Petitot** (G67, G75; R6–8). Among the hardstone boxes made in Dresden is one of cornelian with *Leda and the Swan* on the cover which has a secret panel, rediscovered only in 1976, showing on each side portraits of **Voltaire** and the **marquise du Châtelet** (G80, R27, R28).

This completes the sequence of Galleries.

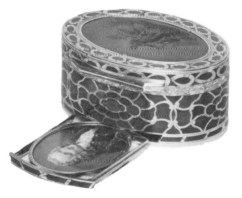

Gold Box with portrait of Voltaire, Dresden (G80)

Index of Artists and Craftsmen mentioned in the text

Reference is made to locations by gallery numbers.

The Seymour-Conway Family
Earls and Marquesses of Hertford

Founders of the Wallace Collection

Francis Seymour-Conway (1719-1794; Earl of Hertford & Viscount Beauchamp 1750; Earl of Yarmouth & *Marquess of Hertford* 1793)

m. 1741 **Lady Isabella Fitzroy** (1726-1782) d. of 2nd Duke of Grafton

seven sons and six daughters, of whom

Francis Ingram Seymour-Conway (1743-1822; Viscount Beauchamp 1750; Earl of Yarmouth 1793; *2nd Marquess of Hertford* 1794)

m. 1. 1768 **Alice Elizabeth** (d.1772); d. of Viscount Windsor

m. 2. 1776 **Isabella Anne Ingram-Shepherd** (1760-1834) d. of 9th Viscount Irvine

only surviving child

Francis Charles Seymour-Conway (1777-1842; Viscount Beauchamp 1793; Earl of Yarmouth 1794; *3rd Marquess of Hertford* 1822)

m. 1798 **Maria Fagnani** (1771-1856)

two sons and a daughter, of whom

Richard Seymour-Conway (1800-1870; Viscount Beauchamp 1800; Earl of Yarmouth 1822; *4th Marquess of Hertford* 1842)

one illegitimate son (by **Mrs Agnes Jackson**, *neé* Wallace, *c.*1789-1864)

Richard (Jackson) Wallace (1818-1890; name changed to Wallace 1842; Baronet 1871)

m. 1871 **Amélie Julie Castelnau** (1819-1897)

Lady Wallace bequeathed the major part of the family's collection of works of art to the Nation as The Wallace Collection